EARLY DAYS with Jesus

Big Activity Book 2

The Ross Family

Nan Drew · Mum · Dad · Gran Ross · Grandpa Ross · Matthew · ...arry · Ben · Kate · Sparks

Fun to Use Bible Activity Book to help you grow with God

How to use Early Days

Early Days has been designed to help parents to teach simple Bible truths in an exciting and practical way.

Choose a quiet area to work and have the materials (if any) needed for the activity at hand. You will find it most helpful to use the Good News Bible as this is the version that the *Early Days* notes are based upon.

Read the Bible verse and then the story, and try to involve your child as much as possible. Encourage him/her to talk about the reading and the story and add your own comments. Try to help your child understand the theme.

Take time to do the activity for the day, but don't worry if you can't finish it or if you miss a few days. It's better to "get together" every other day for a longer time than to rush every day.

After you have completed the activity, say the prayer at the bottom of the page. Encourage your child to add to this prayer time, perhaps including people or situations that you think are relevant.

= Bible reading   = Prayer

God's Family

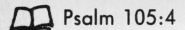 Psalm 105:4

Ben and Kate got up slowly. It was Sunday and there was plenty of time. But suddenly it was time to go! Ben couldn't find his shoe, Kate needed to have her hair brushed and Matthew still had breakfast all over his face!

Find Ben's shoe in this picture.

 Dear Jesus, please help me to hurry when time is short.

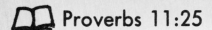 Proverbs 11:25

At last they were ready. While Mum put Matthew in the car, Ben went to knock next door for Mrs Lloyd. During the week Mum took Mrs Lloyd shopping, and on Sundays they always gave her a lift to church.

Colour in and cut out door (see back of book – 1). Hinge and Stick.

 Dear Jesus, please show me ways I can help other people.

Ephesians 1:4-5

Dad had gone off early to help get the church ready. There were chairs and hymn books to put out, the screen to put up and the communion table and lectern to get ready.

Colour in and cut out furniture (see back of book – 2). Stick to picture

Thank You, God, for people who help in church.

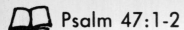 Psalm 47:1-2

The family found four seats at the end of a row, with room for Matthew's pushchair next to them. The music group led two choruses, then after a prayer the pastor told the children the story of Samuel in the Temple.

Draw dot to dot (follow arrows).

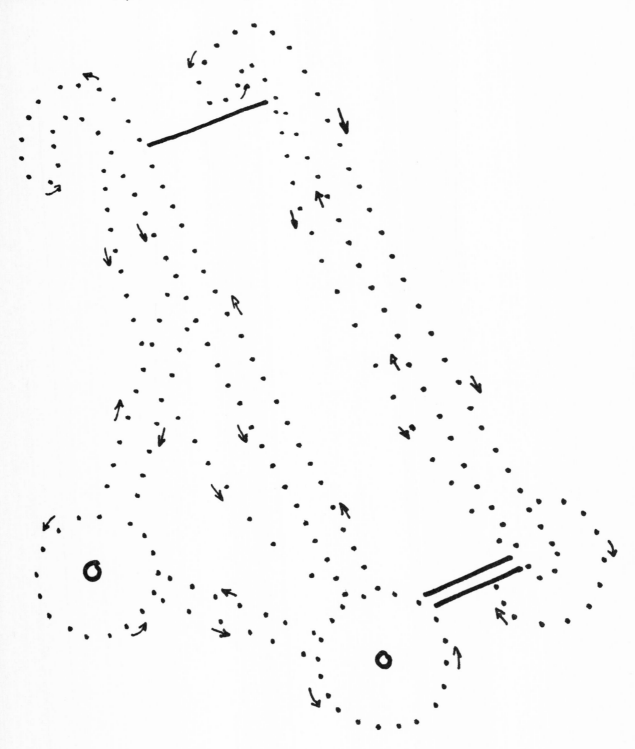

 Lord Jesus, I'm glad that we can sing to You.

📖 1 Samuel 1:11, 19–20

Hannah prayed to God: "Don't forget me! If you give me a son, I promise that I will dedicate him to you for his whole life." The Lord answered Hannah's prayer. She gave birth to a son. She named him Samuel and explained, "I asked the Lord for him."

Colour in

 Thank You, God, that You answer our prayers.

1 Samuel 1:24–28

When Samuel was old enough to eat food, Hannah took him to Eli the priest at Shiloh. Hannah said to Eli, "Do you remember me? I am the woman you saw standing here, praying to the Lord. I asked him for this child, and he gave me what I asked for. So I am dedicating him to the Lord. As long as he lives, he will belong to the Lord."

Colour in

Dear Jesus, help me to keep my promises.

1 Samuel 2:18–19

As Samuel grew up he served the Lord in the Temple. Each year his mother would make a robe and take it to him, when she went with her husband to offer **the yearly sacrifice.**

Colour in

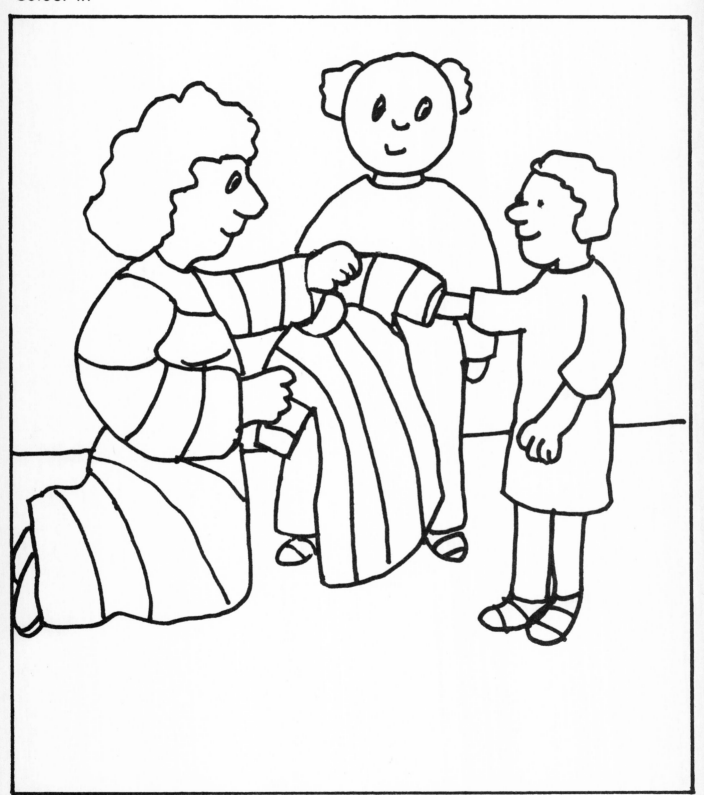

 Thank You, God, for my Mum.

📖 1 Samuel 3:2–10

One night Samuel heard a voice. It was God calling him. Samuel had never heard God before so he thought it was Eli the priest. God called two more times. Each time Samuel went to Eli. The third time Eli said, "It must be God calling; next time, Samuel, say, 'Speak Lord, Your servant is listening.'" The next time God spoke, Samuel said the words and God answered.

Colour in

 Dear God, thank You for speaking to us through the Bible.

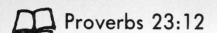 **Proverbs 23:12**

After the children's talk Ben and Kate went out into Sunday School. Mum took Matthew into the creche.

Draw a picture of your Sunday School teacher.

 Thank You, God, for our Sunday School teachers.

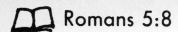 Romans 5:8

This Sunday it was also communion. It was Dad's turn to pass around the bread and the little glasses of grape juice. The communion reminds Christians of Jesus' last supper and that Jesus died for us.

On a large sheet of paper make a collage of a loaf of bread using coloured paper and scraps torn from magazines etc.

 Dear Jesus, thank You for dying for me.

Matthew 26:26–28

Jesus was having supper with the disciples. He broke a piece of bread, said a prayer of thanks and gave it to them. He also gave them a cup of wine to share. The bread was to remind them of His body and the drink of His blood, because He would soon die so that our sins could be forgiven.

Colour in

Dear Jesus, help me not to forget that You died for me.

📖 Psalm 27:1

After the service and Sunday School, Mum and Dad chatted to friends over coffee while the children played outside. When it was time to leave, Kate was nowhere to be found. But after a big search Dad found her helping Mrs Lloyd to wash up in the kitchen.

Which line will find Kate?

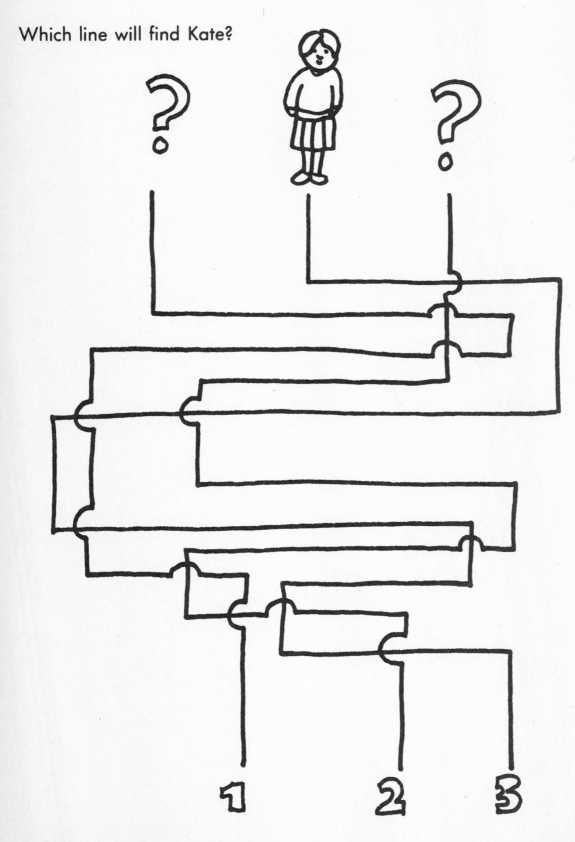

 Dear Jesus, please keep me from getting lost.

Luke 2:41–45

When Jesus was 12 He went with His parents to the festival in Jerusalem. When the festival was over, Jesus stayed, but His parents didn't know this. They thought He was going back home with family or friends. They got worried when they couldn't find Him, so they went back to Jerusalem to look for Him.

Colour in

Father God, help me to remember not to go off on my own without Mum or Dad.

Luke 2:46–51

Jesus' parents found Him in the Temple after a long search. They were astonished to find Him talking with the Jewish teachers. They asked Him why He had stayed behind. Jesus told them He thought they would know He would be in His Father's house, but they didn't understand. He went back home with His parents and obeyed them.

Colour in

 Dear Jesus, help me to be obedient.

 Acts 2:46

Once home from church, Mum soon had the lunch on the table. Mrs Lloyd was eating with them and so was Mike. Mike was a student who had just started at the local college.

Draw your favourite lunch.

 Thank You, God, for meals together.

 Psalm 25:16

It was Mike's first time away from home and he missed his local church. His church was very small and met in the local community centre. There was no one to play the piano, but one of the leaders sang with a guitar.

Two of each of the instruments are the same. Colour in the two that are the same.

 Dear Jesus, please be with people away from home.

Psalm 24:1

As soon as lunch was over, the table cleared and the washing up done, Dad took Matthew upstairs for his sleep. Mum and Mrs Lloyd sat down for a chat, and then Dad and Mike took the children down to the park.

Find six differences in the pictures.

Thank You, God, for outings.

📖 Romans 5:10-11

At the park Ben saw Guy, a new boy from his class at school. They played on the swings and slide while the Dads and Mike chatted. When it was time to go home, Ben asked if Guy could come to Boys' Brigade with him the next evening.

Cut slot to slide Ben and Guy (see back of book – 3).

 Thank You, God, for friends.

📖 Colossians 2:6

It was good at Boys' Brigade. They marched, played games, made models and had a Bible story and quiz. At the end, Captain reminded the boys that it was parade next Sunday. Guy wanted to know why they all went to church. Ben explained that church is where people who know and love Jesus like a friend meet, because they want to spend time with Him there.

Cut out, colour in. Bend tags to dress.

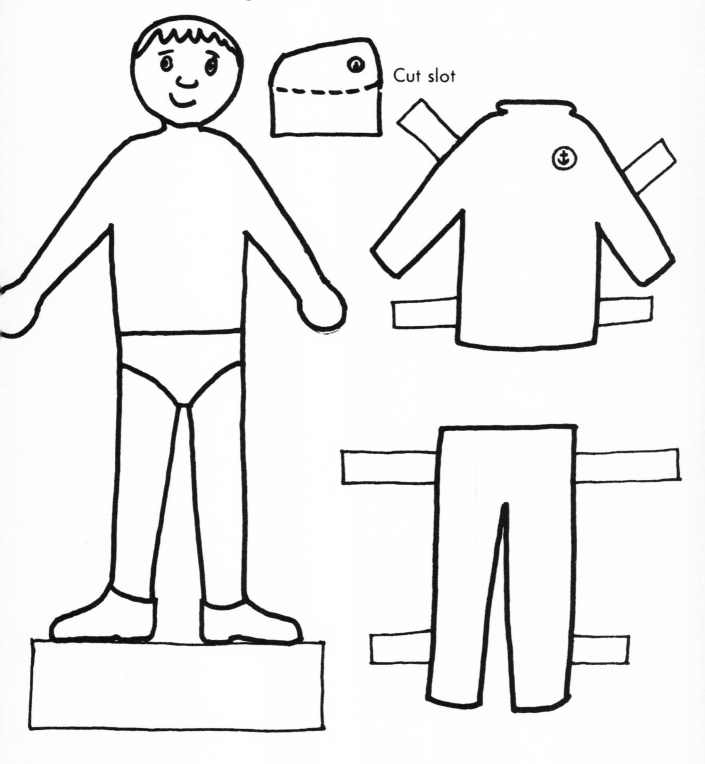

Cut slot

 Dear Jesus, I'm glad I can spend time with You.

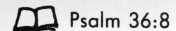 Psalm 36:8

While Ben was at school and Kate was at playgroup, Mum took Matthew to the toddler club at the church. He had a great time, crawling around while the older ones rode bikes and did 'cutting and sticking'. Mum met Mrs Patel, who had just moved into the area. She invited her and her husband to the church picnic.

Cut out shapes to make a jigsaw.

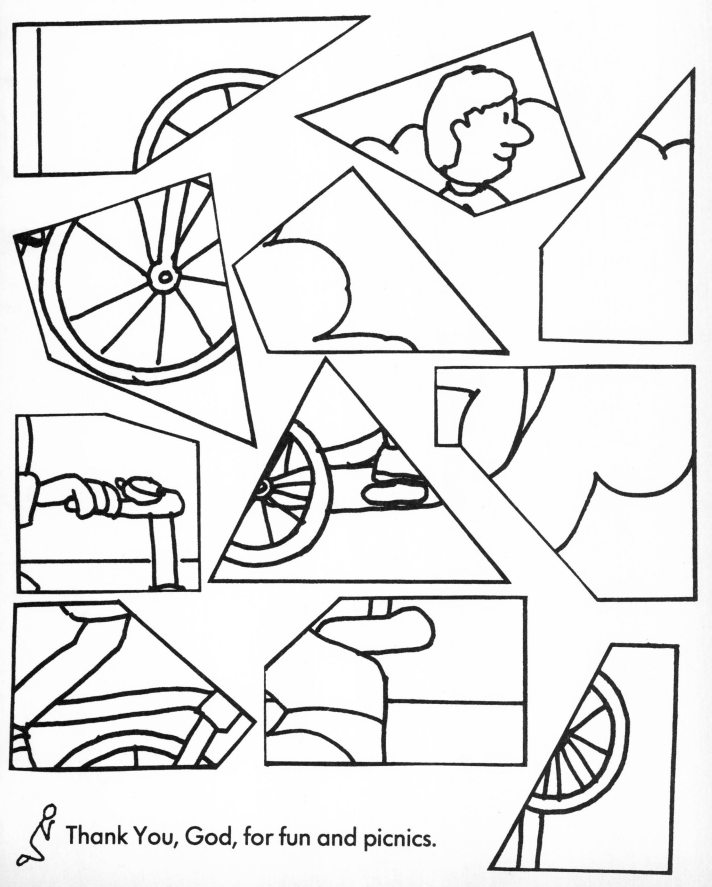

Thank You, God, for fun and picnics.

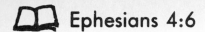 Ephesians 4:6

Next Sunday the Ross family visited their grandparents and cousin Jo was there for the weekend, too. Jo goes to boarding school because her parents are missionaries in Africa. Gran and Grandpa live in a small village and their church is very old. The bells call everyone to church.

Help the Ross family get to church.

 Thank You, God, for different churches.

Psalm 25:4-5

A cross was carried in front of the vicar and the choir as they walked into church. Behind them came the Guides and Scouts, parading just like in B.B. Before the children went out to Junior Church there was a christening. The children crowded around the font to watch. The parents and godparents promised to teach the baby, as he grew, about God and His love. Then the vicar sprinkled water on the baby's forehead.

Trace onto greaseproof or tracing paper and colour with felt tip pens to make stained glass window.

Dear God, please help children like me to learn about You.

📖 Psalm 115:13

Ben and Kate then went out into the hall for Junior Church. After the sermon the vicar blessed the bread and wine, and the Junior Church came back in for communion. Everyone went up to kneel at the altar rail. The vicar gave the bread to the adults and blessed the children, while Grandpa, who was a lay preacher, followed behind with the wine.

Draw a picture of the building in which you worship.

Thank You, God, for your blessing.

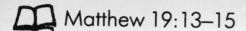 Matthew 19:13–15

Some parents brought their children to Jesus for Him to pray for them. But the disciples tried to send them away. Jesus said, "Let the children come to me, because the Kingdom of Heaven belongs to such as these." Then He blessed them.

Colour in

 Thank You, Jesus, that I can come to You.

Galatians 6:10

After the service everyone stood chatting in the churchyard. Mum and Dad met lots of old friends and some people asked Jo about her Mum and Dad. Gran came out after putting fresh water in the flowers, and Grandpa arranged to go around and cut Mrs Gray's hedge. Then home for lunch!

Stick on scraps of coloured paper on to the flowers.

Thank You, God, for family and friends.

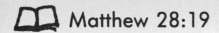 Matthew 28:19

There was so much to talk about. Jo said that when she was with her Mum and Dad in Africa for the holidays, they had a baptismal service. Three new Christians were baptised in the river. They went right under the water and up again. It had been an exciting service and lots of people who didn't know Jesus came to watch.

Finger paint a riverside scene.

 Dear Jesus, please let everyone have a chance to know about You.

Matthew 3:13–17

Jesus asked John to baptise Him in the river Jordan. But John said, "You ought to baptise me." Jesus replied, "God wants you to baptise Me." So John did, and as Jesus was coming out of the water the Holy Spirit came down on Him in the form of a dove. A voice from Heaven said, "This is My own dear Son. I am very pleased with Him."

Colour in

Dear God, help me to please You.

Psalm 22:9

At home the family talked about Matthew's dedication plans. It would be good if all the family could be there. Maybe it could be when Auntie Kath and Uncle Jack were coming back from Africa on holiday. The Rosses' church had dedications instead of christenings. In this service they would say thank you to God for Matthew, and the church and family would promise to tell him about Jesus.

Colour in quilt, stick on cut straws or matchsticks for cot.

Thank You, God, for new babies.

📖 Luke 2:22–23; 27–28

Joseph and Mary took baby Jesus to the Temple in Jerusalem to dedicate Him to God. Simeon, who loved God, was there. The Holy Spirit had told him to go to the Temple. Simeon took Jesus in his arms and thanked God for Him.

Colour in

 Dear Jesus, help me to remember to say thank you.

 Ephesians 2:19

We are all part of God's family when we love Jesus, and so there are many friends in church who can help us learn more about Him.

Colour in

 Thank You, God, that we can all be part of Your family.

On the Move

One day when the Ross family walked back from school there was a big lorry parked next door. It belonged to Brian, Mrs Lloyd's son. He delivers biscuits to supermarkets all over the country.

Make a lorry from boxes and toilet rolls.
Paint or stick on windows and a driver.

 Dear Jesus, please take care of long distance lorry drivers.

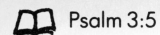 Psalm 3:5

Not long after the family got home, Nan arrived to take Kate to stay the night. The children liked Nan collecting them as she didn't have a car, so they had to ride on the double decker bus.

Draw people in the bus.

 Thank You, Jesus, for chances to go away to stay.

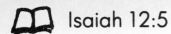 Isaiah 12:5

Ben wasn't going to Nan's because, after tea, he was going with some of the Sunday School to entertain at the Old Folks' Home. He was being collected in the church minibus.

Find the two mini buses that are the same.

 Dear God, please show me how I can help old people.

Psalm 5:11

Next morning Ben was up early. It was the day of his school trip — they were going to a transport museum and at nine o'clock sharp they piled onto the coach.

Help Ben and his class get to the museum.

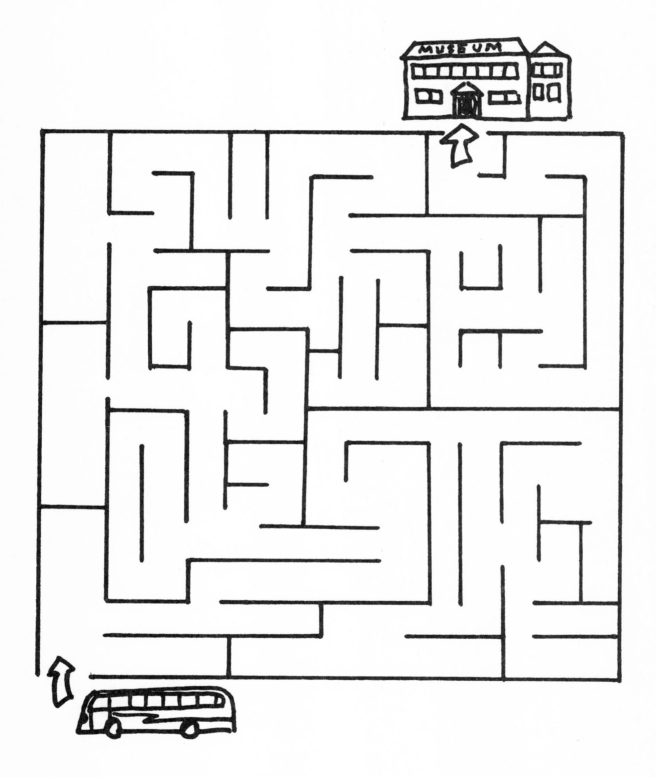

Dear God, please keep people safe as they travel.

At the museum they saw all sorts of old vehicles — carts, carriages, traction engines, steam lorries, bicycles and cars. And the children even had a ride on an old bus.

Make a traction engine out of toilet rolls and card.

Cut hole for funnel.

Cut straws in half and make small holes, push into body for canopy.

Cut toilet roll in half for wheels.

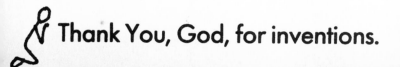

🎵 Thank You, God, for inventions.

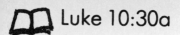 Luke 10:30a

Jesus answered, "There once was a man who was going down from Jerusalem to Jericho."

In Jesus' time there were no cars or buses. Carriages were only for the rich, so most people walked, or rode on donkeys.

Colour in.

 Dear God, help me to remember poor people in other countries.

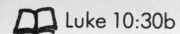 Luke 10:30b

The man was attacked by robbers who "stripped him, and beat him up, leaving him half dead."

Colour in.

 Dear God, please heal people who are hurt.

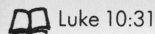 Luke 10:31

"It so happened that a priest was going down that road; but when he saw the man, he walked on by, on the other side."

Colour in.

 Dear Jesus, please forgive me when I don't want to help others.

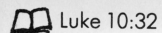 Luke 10:32

"In the same way a Levite also came along, went over and looked at the man, and then walked on by, on the other side."

Colour in

 Dear Jesus, please don't let me turn away from people who need help.

Luke 10:33, 34a

"But a Samaritan who was travelling that way came upon the man, and when he saw him, his heart was filled with pity. He went over to him, poured oil and wine on his wounds and bandaged them."

Colour in.

 Dear Jesus, thank You for doctors and nurses and people who care.

"Then he put the man on his own animal and took him to an inn, where he took care of him. The next day he took out two silver coins and gave them to the innkeeper. 'Take care of him,' he told the innkeeper, 'and when I come back this way, I will pay you whatever else you spend on him.'"

Colour in.

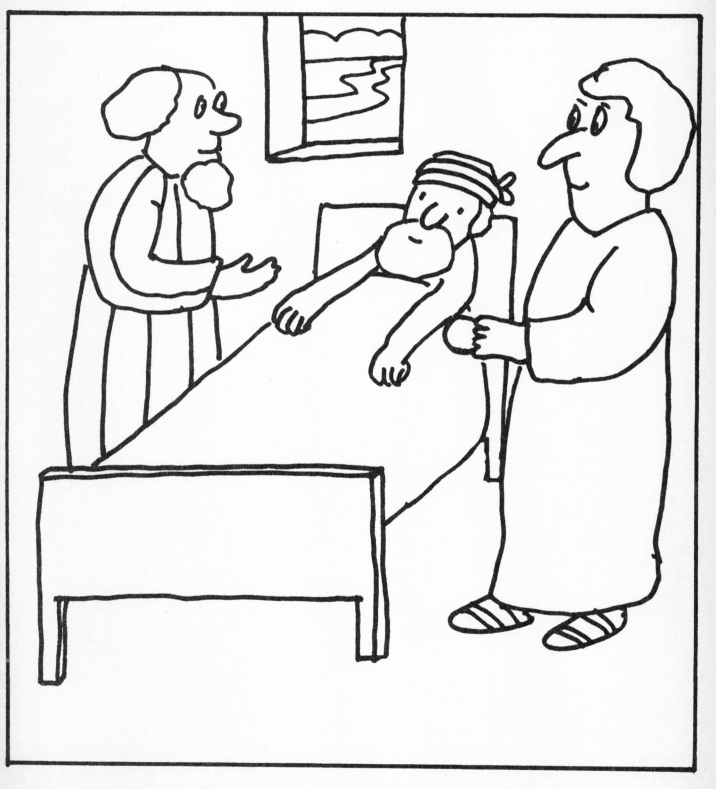

🙏 Dear Jesus, please help me to be kind to others.

How can we help our neighbours?

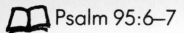 Psalm 95:6–7

Once a week Dad goes to work on his bike so that after dropping Kate at playgroup Mum can go to the supermarket in the car. She usually gives Mrs Lloyd a lift but today she has a cold, so Mum takes her shopping list instead.

Stick on straws, pipe cleaners or wool to make bike.

 Dear God, please take care of old people.

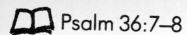 Psalm 36:7–8

Mum has lots to buy at the supermarket because this week the family is off on holiday.

Stick on pictures from magazines or draw
your favourite foods in the trolley.

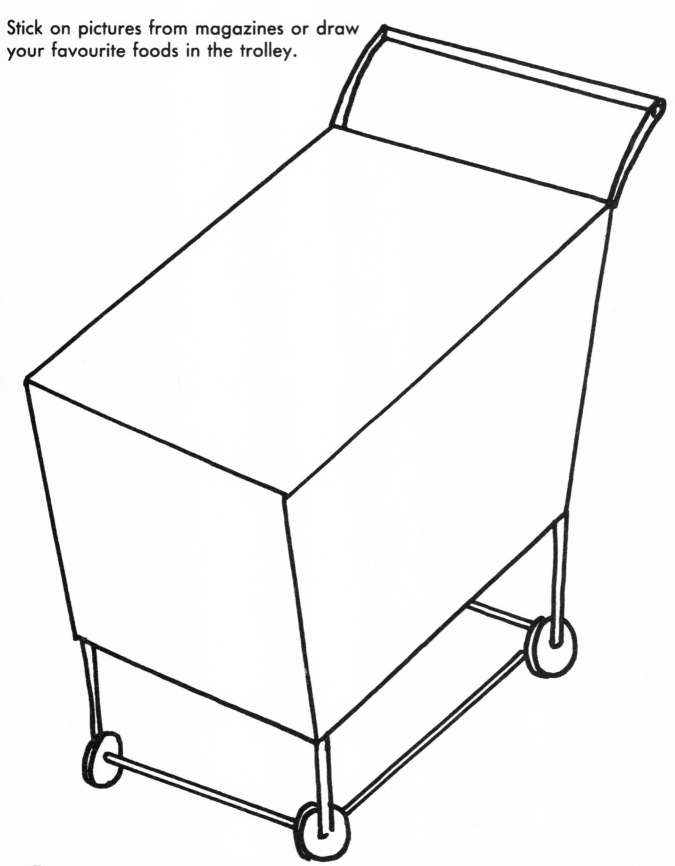

 Dear God, thank You for holidays.

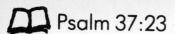 Psalm 37:23

At last everything was packed in the car and the Rosses were ready to go. Mrs Lloyd was looking after Sparks but Barry was going too. They must hurry as they have a boat to catch.

Find six differences in these pictures.

Dear Jesus, thank You for people who care for pets.

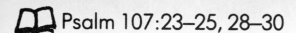 Psalm 107:23–25, 28–30

They reached the ferry in plenty of time and Dad drove on. The children hadn't been on a boat before so they spent the time looking around the deck and watching the water.

Cut slot in sea. (see back of book – 4 – for boat)

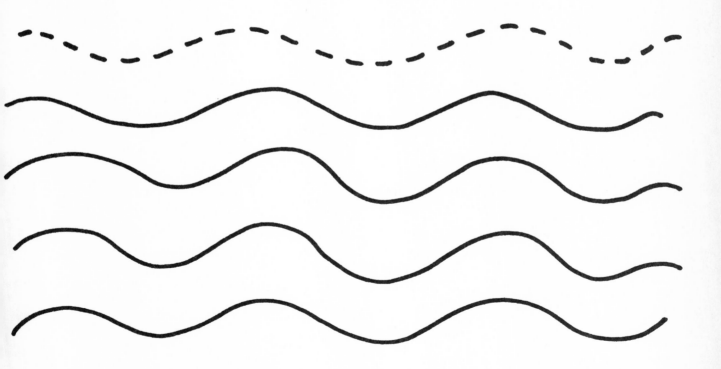

 Dear Jesus, thank You for new adventures.

When they reached the other side, it was not far to drive to the caravan. Then there was all the unpacking to do!

Cut out to make a jigsaw.

 Dear God, help me to be willing to help.

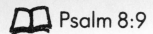 Psalm 8:9

During the holiday the family explored lots of new places, went for some long walks, and one day they even went on an old steam train.

Colour in and stick on wool for smoke.

 Dear God, thank You for new places.

📖 Psalm 33:4

In the evenings they played games. One night they had a quiz.
1. How did the kings come to visit baby Jesus?
2. What did Jesus ride on Palm Sunday?
3. How did Jonah go to Nineveh?
4. In what did Pharaoh chase the Israelites to the Red Sea?
5. What was the covenant box carried on?
6. What was Jesus doing on the road to Emmaus?

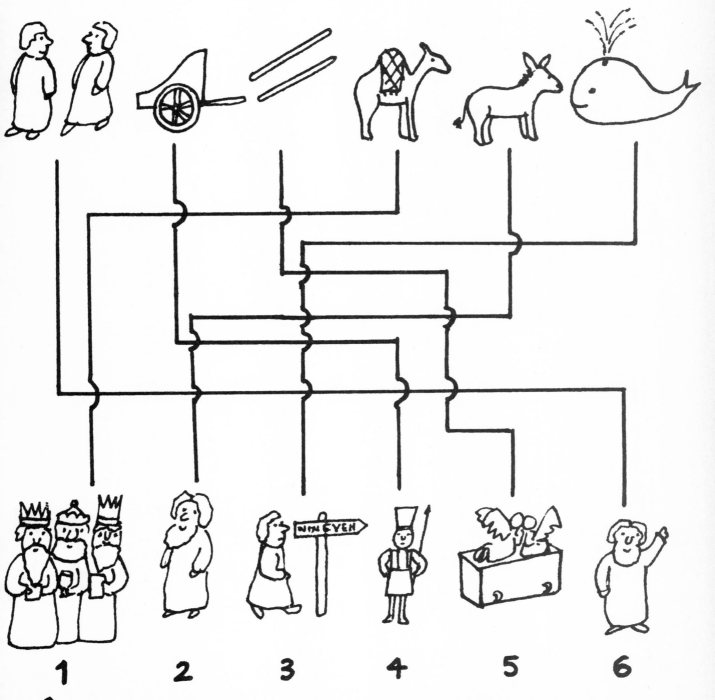

1   2   3   4   5   6

Dear God, help me to get to know the stories in Your Bible.

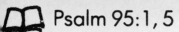 Psalm 95:1, 5

Soon the holiday was over but there was still a surprise to come. Instead of going back on the ferry, Dad had booked the car on the hovercraft! It skimmed across the water so quickly they were soon on the other side!

Cut slot in sea to move hovercraft. (see back of book – 5 – for Hovercraft)
You could make a sea and harbour scene
on a large sheet of paper. Cut slots and use
the boat and the hovercraft.

 Dear God, thank You for surprises.

Instead of going straight home the family decided to stop off at Gran and Grandpa's farm. Cousin Jo was there from boarding school.

Help the Ross family to find the right road to the farm.

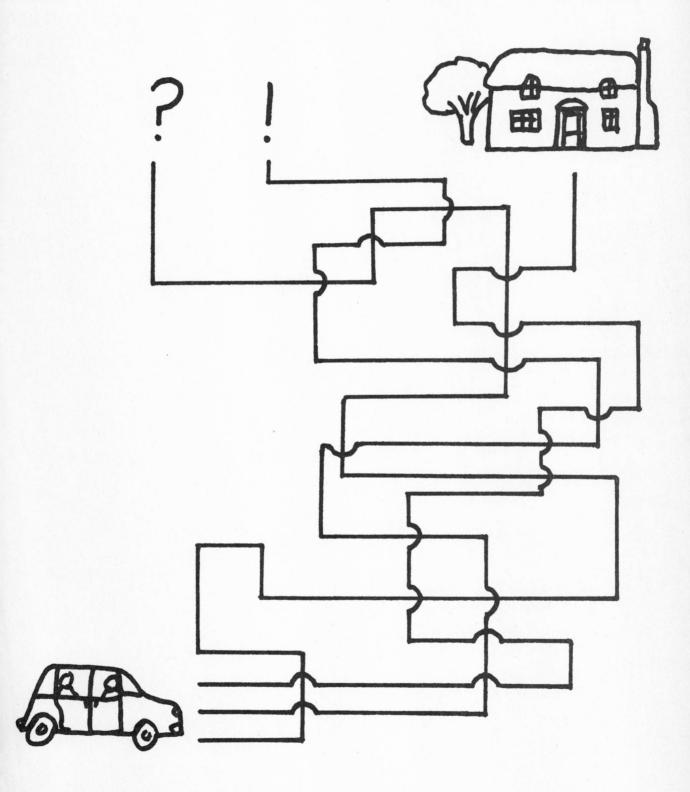

 Dear God, thank You for grandparents.

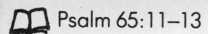 Psalm 65:11–13

After church and a big lunch Grandpa let all the bigger cousins ride on the trailer when he took a tank of water up to the sheep in the top field.

Draw the children on the trailer.

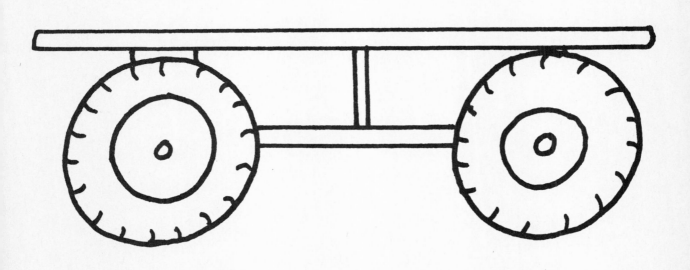

 Dear God, thank You that we have plenty of water and help me to remember those who haven't.

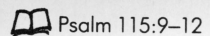 Psalm 115:9–12

Next day Dad left early as he had to get back to work and on the way drop Jo at the airport. She is flying to Kenya to join Uncle Jack, Auntie Kath, Paul and Andy for the holidays.

Cut slot to fly plane. (see back of book – 6 – for plane)

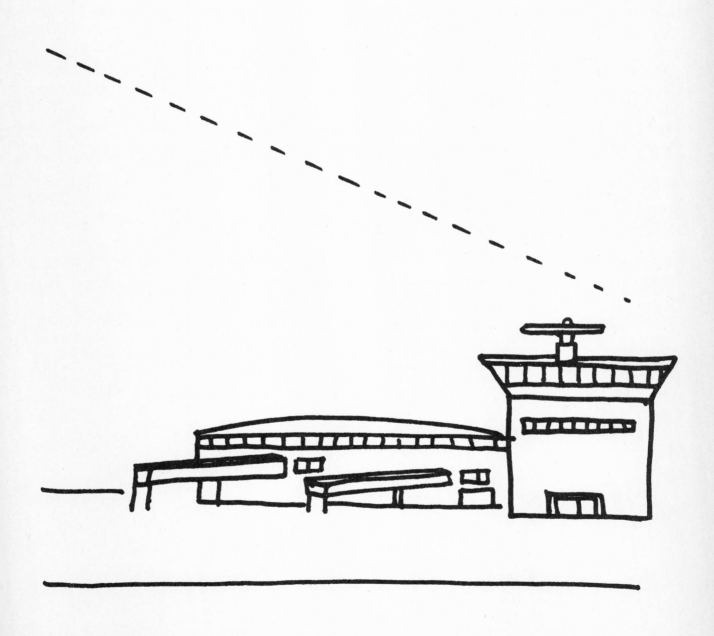

 Dear God, please take care of our family when we have to be apart.

Soon it was time for Mum and the children to go home too. Grandad took them to the station. It was great fun on the train — so much to see and Daddy came to meet them at the other end.

Colour in cut-out. Stick together, crease to make concertina and pull.

🙏 Dear Jesus, thank You for families.

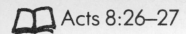 Acts 8:26–27

"An angel of the Lord said to Philip, 'Get ready and go south to the road that goes from Jerusalem to Gaza.' (This road is not used nowadays.) So Philip got ready and went."

Colour in.

Dear God, please let everyone have a chance to hear about You.

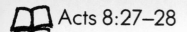 Acts 8:27–28

"Now an Ethiopian eunuch, who was an important official in charge of the treasury of the queen of Ethiopia, was on his way home. He had been to Jerusalem to worship God and was going back home in his carriage."

Colour in.

 Dear God, thank You for Your book, the Bible.

📖 Acts 8:29–30

"The Holy Spirit said to Philip, 'Go over to that carriage and stay close to it.' Philip ran over and heard him reading from the book of the prophet Isaiah. He asked him, 'Do you understand what you are reading?'"

Colour in.

 Dear God, help me to understand Your Book.

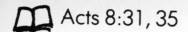 Acts 8:31, 35

"The official replied, 'How can I understand unless someone explains it to me?'...Then Philip began to speak; starting from this passage of scripture, he told him the Good News about Jesus."

Colour in.

Dear God, thank You for people who explain Your Book to me.

📖 Acts 8:36, 38

"As they travelled down the road, they came to a place where there was some water, and the official said, 'Here is some water. What is to keep me from being baptised?' The official ordered the carriage to stop, and both Philip and the official went down into the water, and Philip baptised him."

Colour in.

 Dear God, please help me to do what I am told.

📖 Psalm 16:2

Back home Ben and Kate went out to play while Mum unpacked the cases and sorted out the washing. Soon they were racing up and down the road, Ben on his scooter followed by Kate on her tricycle.

Draw from dot to dot

 Thank You, God, for my toys.

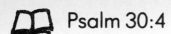 Psalm 30:4

Whilst Matthew had his rest, Ben and Kate helped Mum sort out their souvenirs: a postcard of the hovercraft, tickets from the old train and lots of photos. What a lot of ways to travel. Which other ones can you remember?

Draw some ways that we can travel
or stick on pictures from magazines.

 Thank You, God, for all the ways we travel.

My Home

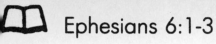 Ephesians 6:1-3

Ben and Dad came in carrying rolls of paper and pots of paint. They were going to start on what was going to be the boys' room.

Cut out to
make picture.

 Thank You, God, for times with Dad.

Baby Matthew was getting too big for Mum and Dad's room and he was going to move in with Ben. Ben wasn't too keen. He had got used to having his own room since they moved from the flat.

Cut out the finger puppet and colour-in. Cut a matchbox as shown. Place finger in box.

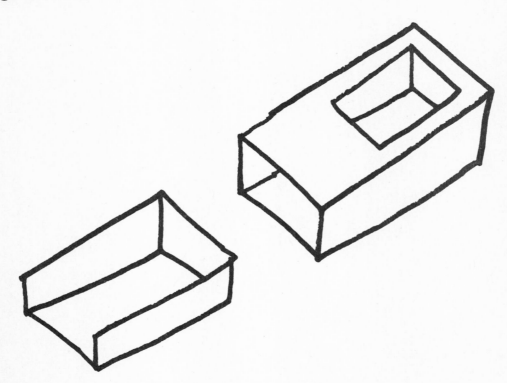

 Dear Jesus, please help me to learn to share.

Meanwhile, during the decorating Ben slept in a sleeping bag on Kate's floor. That was fun. It was a bit like indoor camping, but Ben didn't think he would want to do it all the time!

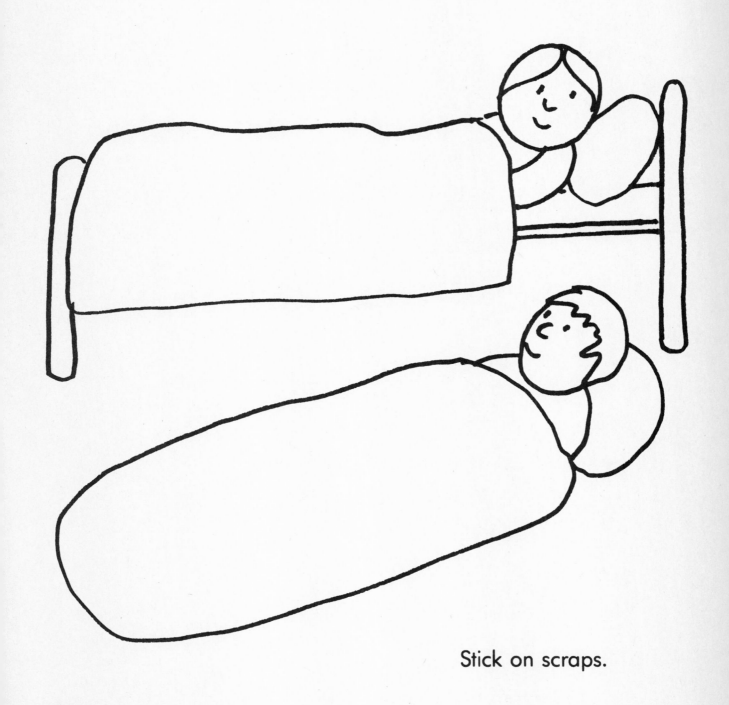

Stick on scraps.

 Thank You, God, for 'fun times'.

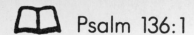 Psalm 136:1

Ben was going to have a new bed. He was going to sleep high up, over the top of his dressing table. At least Matthew couldn't reach his things up there!

Colour in the shapes with dots in to make the picture.

 **Thank You, God, for new things.**

After tea Dad came and sat down next to Ben. He started talking about their old flat. Did Ben and Kate remember how they had to sit and eat in the living room, and if someone came to see Dad they had to go into the kitchen? When Mum and Dad had a meeting they had to go to bed early and miss the television.

What would you find in a kitchen?

Thank You, God, for times to talk to each other.

📖 John 14:1-3

Ben began to think. At the flat there had only been two bedrooms. He and Kate had had to share. Here they had a lounge and dining room and a nice garden to play in. Perhaps sharing with Matthew wouldn't be so bad.

Make a picture of a living room by cutting out pictures from magazines.

 Thank You, God, for my house.

The more Ben, Kate and Dad talked, the more they realised what they had. Kate's friend, Sarah, had to share a bedroom with two brothers and a boy in Ben's class shared with twin babies!

Which children share which room? Follow lines to find out.

Dear Jesus, please help me to remember people who don't have as much as I do.

Sometimes we find it hard not to always want more. Jesus can help us learn to be content with what we have.

nd six differences in these pictures.

Dear Jesus, please help me learn to be content.

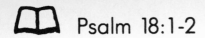 Psalm 18:1-2

There are lots of people who live in only one room. Often they have to share the kitchen and bathroom with other families.

Draw from dot to dot.

 **Dear Jesus, please be with people who don't have much room.**

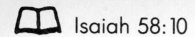 Isaiah 58:10

Some people have nowhere to live and end up sleeping in shop doorways or on park benches.

Cut out and stick on person (see back of book – 7).

 **Dear Jesus, please take care of people who have nowhere to sleep.**

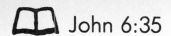 John 6:35

Mum reminded the children of the places Auntie Kath and Uncle Jack talked about. Ecuador was one, where many people only have one small meal a day and have to buy water for drinking and washing.

Help the people to get to the water.

 Dear Jesus, please help me to remember people who do not have much to eat.

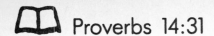 Proverbs 14:31

They also spoke of Southern Africa, where many poor people live in shacks made out of flattened oil drums and fetch water from taps a long way from their homes.

Stick on silver paper for water.

 Dear Jesus, please help me not to waste water just because it is there.

📖 Lamentations 3:22-23

Ben and Kate began to realise how well off they are. They have a nice house, a cosy bed and plenty to eat. (What else can you think of?)

Draw a picture of your home.

Dear Jesus, please help me to realise how well off I am.

Psalm 25:16

Something much more important than *what* you have is *who* you have. A family makes a house into a home. Even if you have a lovely house and plenty of nice things, life can be very sad and lonely if you are alone.

Draw a picture of your family.

Thank You, God, for my home.

 Romans 8:37-39

It is good to know that we are never completely alone.
Jesus is always with us, even if we feel lonely, cold, hungry
or just fed up.

Colour-in.

Thank You, Jesus, that I have You.

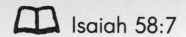 Isaiah 58:7

Ben felt much happier about sharing his bedroom now. After all, he did love Matthew and it was fun helping Dad to paint the doors.

Cut slot, cut out arm to paint (see back of book – 8).

 Thank You, God, for the fun of helping.

King Solomon decided to build a house to worship God – it was called the Temple. It was not very big but very beautiful – nothing but the best for God. 80,000 men quarried the stone and 70,000 carried it.

Colour-in.

 Thank You, God, for people who work for You.

📖 2 Chronicles 2:16

The best trees grew in Lebanon, so Solomon arranged for them to be cut and made into rafts to be sent down the coast by sea to Israel.

Colour-in.

 **Thank You, God, for trees.**

📖 2 Chronicles 3:3-14

In the Temple there were two rooms. The inner one was very dark – that was where they kept God's laws in a special box made of wood and covered with gold.

Colour-in.

 Dear God, please help me to keep Your laws.

The outer room of the Temple was bigger. It was covered in gold and beautiful carvings. There was an altar and ten lampstands.

Colour-in.

 Thank You, God, for beautiful things.

It is always important to give God the best but often people forget and think of themselves first. Then things go wrong. Hundreds of years after Solomon, God's Temple was in ruins and He sent this message to the people: "My people, why should you be living in well-built houses while my Temple lies in ruins?"

Colour-in.

 Dear Jesus, please help me to remember to put You first.

"You have sown much corn, but have harvested very little. You have food to eat, but not enough to make you full . . . You have clothing, but not enough to keep you warm. And the working man cannot earn enough to live on . . . Now go up into the hills, get timber, and rebuild the Temple."

Colour-in.

Dear Jesus, please help people who don't have enough food and clothes.

John 8:12

Before Jesus was born the people felt that they had to go to the Temple to be close to God. Now we know that although it is good to go to church and share with other people, we can be close to God anywhere.

Stick on pillars (see back of book – 9).

 Thank You, God, that You are close to us always.

Matthew 6:6a, 7a, 8b

Jesus tells us how to talk to God.

"When you pray, go to your room, close the door, and pray to your Father, who is unseen . . . When you pray, do not use a lot of meaningless words . . . Your Father already knows what you need before you ask him."

Colour-in.

Thank You, God, for knowing what I need.

The boys' room was finished. It looked good – there was footballer wallpaper and a football lampshade. Ben was even pleased when Mum and Dad moved Matthew's cot in.

Cut out cot (see back of book – 10) and stick on. Where do you think it should be?

Thank You, God, for my bedroom.

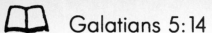

Mum was very surprised when Ben asked if Auntie Kath and Uncle Jack could use his room when they came to stay. Why? Because he was so pleased with it he wanted to share it with them too!

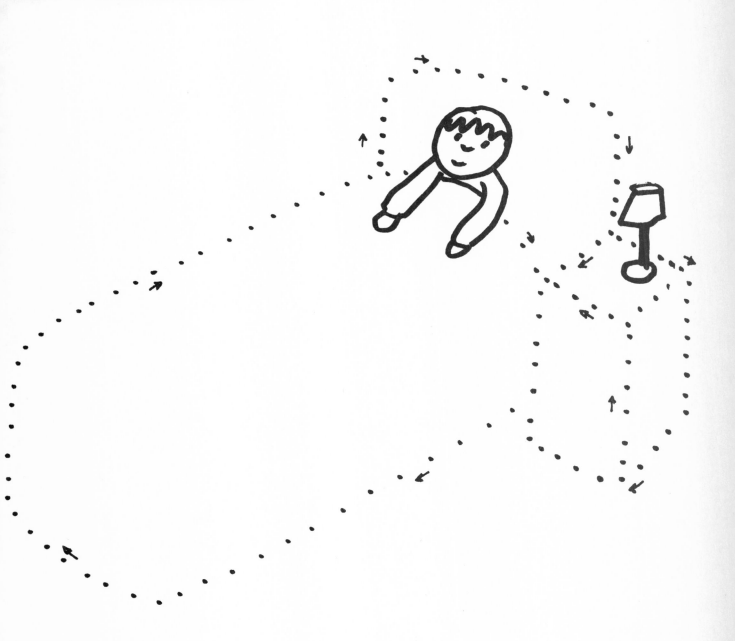

Draw from dot to dot.

 Thank You, God, that I have things to share.

"Then the Lord said to Elijah, 'Now go to the town of Zarephath, near Sidon, and stay there. I have commanded a widow who lives there to feed you.' So Elijah went to Zarephath, and as he came to the gate of the town, he saw a widow gathering firewood. 'Please bring me a drink of water,' he said to her. And as she was going to get it, he called out, 'And please bring me some bread, too.'"

Colour-in.

 Thank You, God, that I can talk to You.

1 Kings 17:12

"She answered, 'By the living Lord your God I swear that I haven't got any bread. All I have is a handful of flour in a bowl and a drop of olive-oil in a jar. I came here to gather some firewood to take back home and prepare what little I have for my son and me. That will be our last meal, and then we will starve to death.'"

Colour-in.

Dear Jesus, please take care of people who are hungry.

"'Don't worry,' Elijah said to her. 'Go ahead and prepare your meal. But first make a small loaf from what you have and bring it to me, and then prepare the rest for you and your son. For this is what the Lord, the God of Israel, says: 'The bowl will not run out of flour or the jar run out of oil before the day that I, the Lord, send rain.'"

Colour-in.

 Dear Jesus, please help me to do what You tell me.

📖 1 Kings 17: 15-16

"The widow went and did as Elijah had told her, and all of them had enough food for many days. As the Lord had promised through Elijah, the bowl did not run out of flour nor did the jar run out of oil."

Isn't it good to know that if we are willing to share what we have, we are not only making other people happy but God happy too!

Colour-in.

 Dear Jesus, help me to make You happy.

The Party

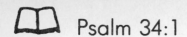 Psalm 34:1

Kate was very excited when she came out of play group. She had a party invitation. Sarah was going to have a fancy dress party and Kate was invited to go.

Help Kate by designing her invite. You could draw in felt tips or crayons and stick on pictures from magazines.

 Thank You, God, for invitations.

📖 Psalm 8:1-2a

Mum checked on the calendar – yes, Kate could go. So she wrote the acceptance and took it back to play group.

Colour-in.

 Thank You, God, for exciting times.

Luke 14:16b and 17

"There was once a man who was giving a great feast to which he invited many people. When it was time for the feast, he sent his servant to tell his guests, 'Come, everything is ready!'"

Colour-in.

 Thank You, God, for the fun of getting ready.

Luke 14:18

"But they all began, one after another, to make excuses. The first one told the servant, 'I have bought a field and must go and look at it; please accept my apologies.'"

Colour-in.

Dear Jesus, please forgive me when I can't do something.

Luke 14:19

"Another one said, 'I have bought five pairs of oxen and am on my way to try them out; please accept my apologies.'"

Colour-in.

 Dear Jesus, please help me not to make excuses.

📖 Luke 14:20

"Another one said, 'I have just got married, and for that reason I cannot come.'"

Colour-in.

 Dear Jesus, please help me to tell the truth.

"The servant went back and told all this to his master. The master was furious and said to his servant, 'Hurry out to the streets and alleys of the town, and bring back the poor, the crippled, the blind, and the lame.'"

Colour-in.

 Dear Jesus, please help me to think of others.

Luke 14:22-23

"Soon the servant said, 'Your order has been carried out, sir, but here is room for more.' So the master said to the servant, 'Go out to the country roads and lanes and make people come in, so that my house will be full.'"

Colour-in.

Dear Jesus, please show me how I can share what I have with other people.

Kate had thought a lot about the party and what she wanted to be – a clown, a cowboy, an angel, a rabbit, or maybe a flower. Finally, Mum and Kate decided she should go as a cat.

Cut out and colour-in.

Thank You, God, for the fun of dressing up.

Kate could wear her leotard from dancing, her black tights and Ben's balaclava. All they needed to get was some felt for the ears, wool for a tail and face paint to draw the whiskers, so off they went to the shops.

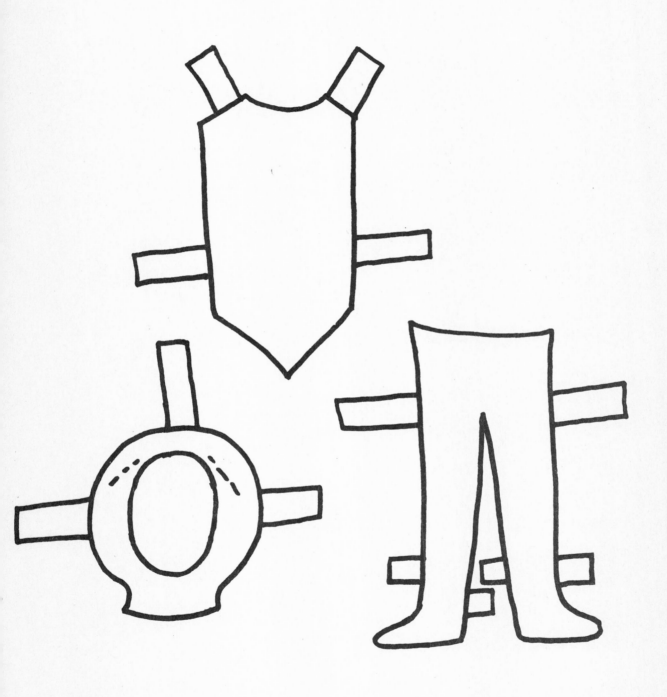

Cut out and colour-in.

 Thank You, God, for good ideas.

Mum sewed on the ears after she had shown Kate how to plait the tail. Then Mum asked Kate if she had any ideas for a present. Sarah liked dolls, books and playing games but Kate didn't think she was very keen on puzzles.

Cut out and colour-in
(see back of book – 11 – for other costumes).

 **Thank You, God, for Mums who help us.**

James 1:17

Before Mum and Kate went to collect Ben from school, Mum put Matthew in the pram and they went down to the toy shop. After a lot of thought, Kate chose a dressing up doll and a colouring book. On the way back they stopped at the paper shop and chose a card. Sarah was going to be four.

Help Kate to get to the toy shop.

Dear Jesus, please help me when I am choosing a present for someone else.

Mum took Kate to the party and then went home. There were lots of children. Kate felt a bit shy but she knew most of them.

Cut out to make the picture.

Dear Jesus, please help me when I'm feeling shy.

Soon the children were playing games: musical chairs, tail on the donkey and farmer's in his den. Kate won pass the parcel – she got a bar of chocolate.

Draw a picture of your favourite game.

Dear Jesus, please help us to enjoy ourselves even though we don't always win.

Kate was the only cat. There were two clowns, a policeman, a nurse and lots of others. Sarah was a beautiful princess.

Draw a line to join up the same costumes.

Thank You, God, for fun.

The children had a lovely tea with crisps, sausages, cakes and jelly. Sarah's Mum had made her cake to look like a butterfly.

Colour in the shapes with dots in them to make the picture.

Thank You, God, for party food.

It was a good party and Kate was really tired by the time Mum came to fetch her. She even had to be reminded to say thank you for her party bag and goodbye to Sarah's Mum. She had had a lovely time.

Draw from dot to dot.

 Dear Jesus, please help me to remember to say thank you.

Birthdays are a time for sharing – presents for the birthday person, a party for everyone and party bags for the guests to take home. Christmas is a time for sharing too.

Stick on the party bags (see back of book – 12).

 Dear Jesus, please help me want to share.

Ben and Kate like to choose the right Christmas card for each person. Kate always looks at the pictures. A kitten for Nan Drew and a snowman for the cousins. They all enjoyed building a snowman together at Gran and Grandpa's. Ben thinks about the words too. Thinking and choosing shows that you care.

Stick on cotton wool.

 Dear Jesus, please help me to care about other people as You do.

What should we buy for Mrs Lloyd? Mum was writing out the present list. She was trying to think of the perfect present for each person. Ben remembered that Mrs Lloyd had lost her gloves last week, so she really did need some new ones.

Find the gloves.

 Teach me, God, to think about other people.

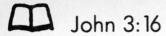 John 3:16

Isn't it fun on Christmas morning opening all your presents? It's also fun to see what everyone else has and especially to watch as they open what you have chosen for them.

Join up the right presents to the right people.

 **Thank You, God, for gifts.**

 Romans 6:23b

God gave us the most perfect gift at Christmas – His Son, Jesus, not just as a baby but to die on the cross for our sins and to live with us always.

Colour-in.

Thank You, God, for giving us Jesus.

The Ross family had another party to look forward to – Gran and Grandpa's ruby wedding. They had been married for 40 years.

Find the six differences.

 Thank You, God, for anniversaries.

📖 Romans 8:28

Mum and Auntie Kath had arranged a surprise party. Lots of friends were coming and even Gran and Grandpa's bridesmaid!

Draw a line to the two bridesmaids who are exactly the same.

 **Thank You, God, for surprises.**

It was very hard to choose the right present. In the end Mum and Dad decided to get a flowering tree for the garden. Gran and Grandpa could enjoy that all the time.

Stick on scraps for blossom.

Dear Jesus, please help me to choose the right presents for people.

It was a lovely party. Gran and Grandpa were surprised. Everyone had a lot to talk about. Kate and Ben liked it most when Gran and Grandpa talked about their wedding and what it was like when they were young. Everything had changed so much.

Colour-in.

 Thank You, God, for times when I can listen.

There was a wedding in the town of Cana in Galilee. Jesus' mother was there, and Jesus and his disciples had also been invited to the wedding.

Colour-in.

 Thank You, God, for wedding parties.

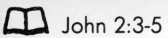 John 2:3-5

When the wine had given out, Jesus' mother said to him, "They have no wine left."

"You must not tell me what to do," Jesus replied. "My time has not yet come."

Jesus' mother then told the servants, "Do whatever he tells you."

Colour-in.

 Dear Jesus, please help me to be obedient.

Jesus said to the servants, "Fill these jars with water." They filled them to the brim, and then he told them, "Now draw some water out and take it to the man in charge of the feast." They took him the water, which now had turned into wine, and he tasted it. He did not know where this wine had come from (but, of course, the servants who had drawn out the water knew) . . .

Colour-in.

 Dear Jesus, please help me when things go wrong.

📖 John 2:9b-10

. . . so he called the bridegroom and said to him, "Everyone else serves the best wine first, and after the guests have had plenty to drink, he serves the ordinary wine. But you have kept the best wine until now!"

Colour-in.

 Thank You, Jesus, for Your miracles.

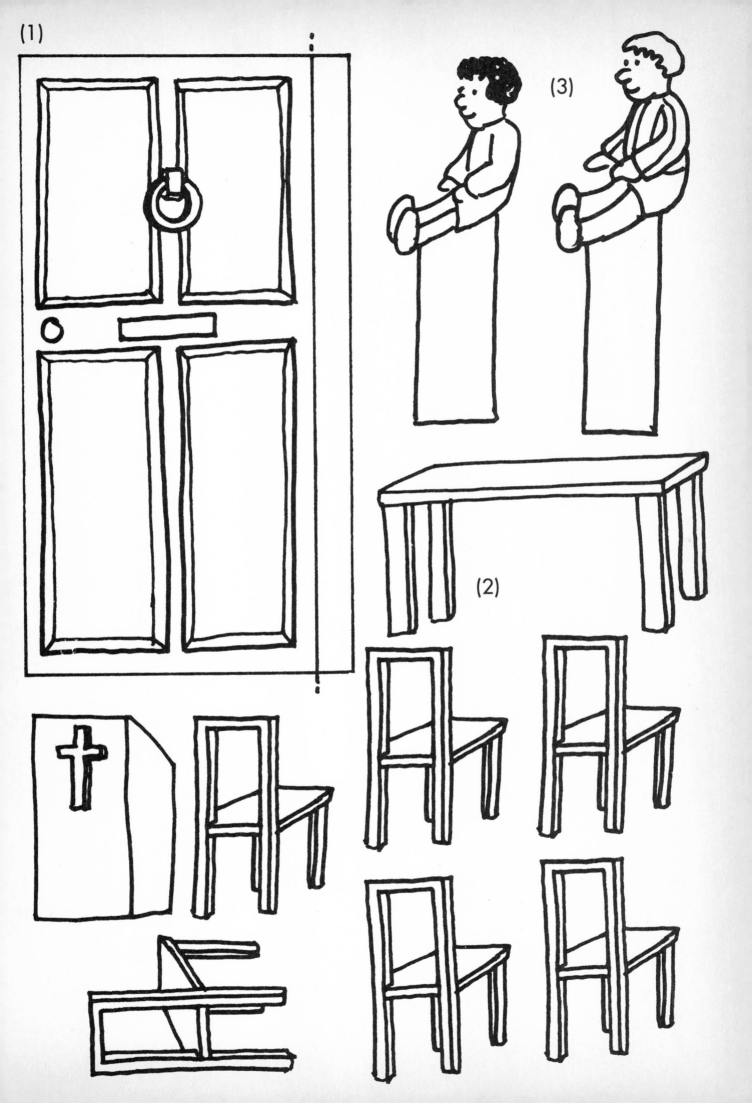

(1)

(3)

(2)

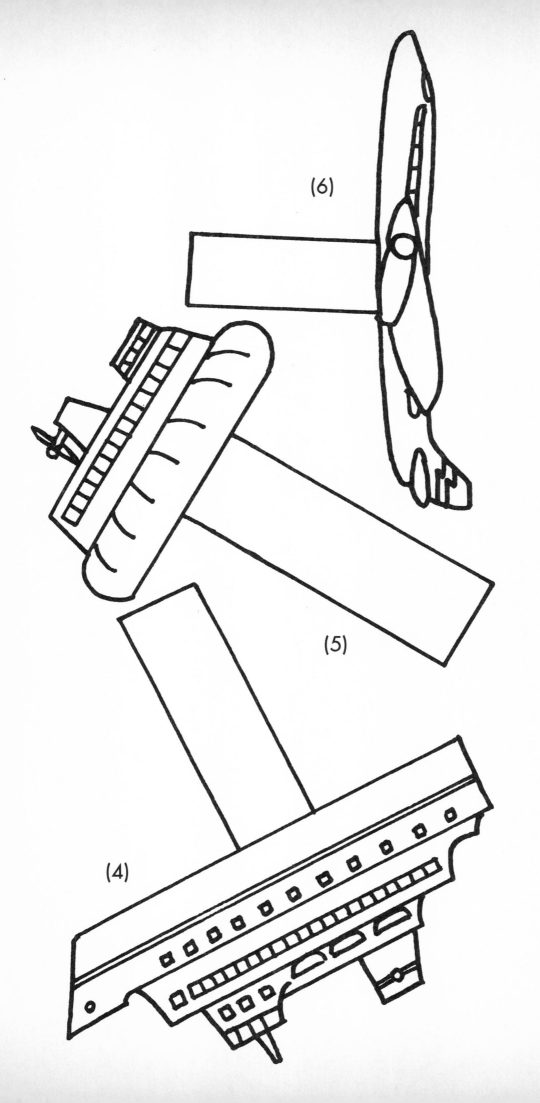

(6)

(5)

(4)

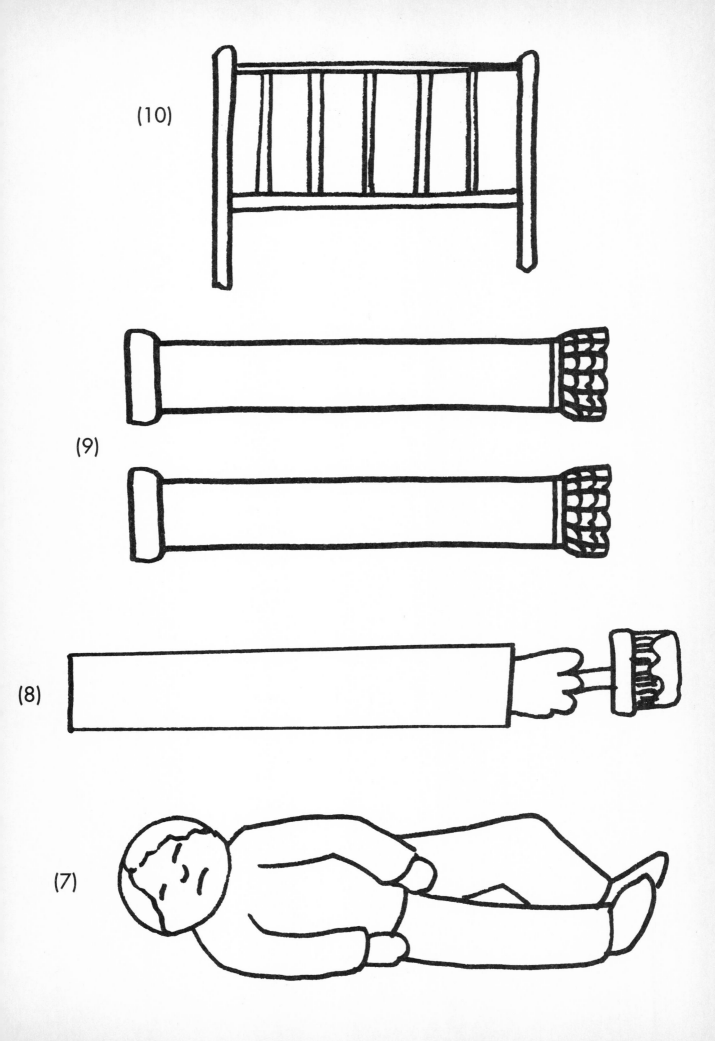

(10)

(9)

(8)

(7)

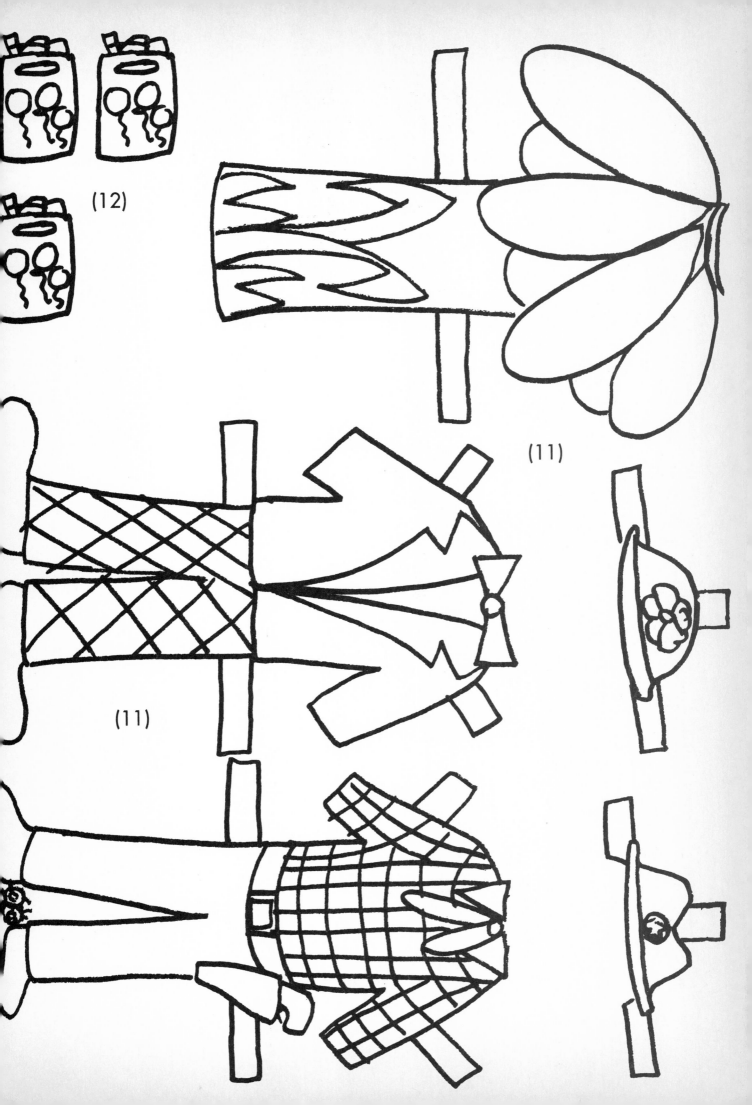

(12)

(11)

(11)